CHANCE THE RAPPER

Making a Difference in Hip-Hop

By Katie Kawa

People Who Make a Difference

Published in 2022 by
KidHaven Publishing, an Imprint of Greenhaven Publishing, LLC
29 E. 21st Street
New York, NY 10010

Designer: Deanna Paternostro
Editor: Katie Kawa

Photo credits: Cover Kevin Mazur/Contributor/Getty Images Entertainment/Getty Images; p. 5 AFP Contributor/Contributor/AFP/Getty Images; p. 7 Chicago Tribune/Contributor/Tribune News Service/Getty Images; p. 9 Barry Brecheisen/Contributor/WireImage/Getty Images; p. 11 Kevork Djansezian/Stringer/Getty Images Entertainment/Getty Images; p. 13 Charley Gallay/Stringer/Getty Images Entertainment/Getty Images; p. 15 Jim Young/Contributor/AFP/Getty Images; p. 17 Joshua Lott/Stringer/Getty Images News/Getty Images; p. 18 Timothy Hiatt/Contributor/Getty Images Entertainment/Getty Images; p. 20 Debra L Rothenberg/Stringer/WireImage/Getty Images; p. 21 T.Sumaetho/Shutterstock.com.

Library of Congress Cataloging-in-Publication Data

Names: Kawa, Katie, author.
Title: Chance the Rapper : making a difference in hip-hop / Katie Kawa.
Description: [First.] | New York : KidHaven Publishing, 2022. | Series: People who make a difference | Includes index.
Identifiers: LCCN 2020034184 | ISBN 9781534536999 (library binding) | ISBN 9781534536975 (paperback) | ISBN 9781534536982 (set) | ISBN 9781534537002 (ebook)
Subjects: LCSH: Chance the Rapper–Juvenile literature. | Rap musicians–United States–Biography–Juvenile literature.
Classification: LCC ML3930.C442 K38 2022 | DDC 782.421649092 [B]–dc23
LC record available at https://lccn.loc.gov/2020034184

Printed in the United States of America

Some of the images in this book illustrate individuals who are models. The depictions do not imply actual situations or events.

CPSIA compliance information: Batch #CW22KH: For further information contact Greenhaven Publishing LLC, New York, New York at 1-844-317-7404.

Please visit our website, www.greenhavenpublishing.com. For a free color catalog of all our high-quality books, call toll free 1-844-317-7404 or fax 1-844-317-7405.

CONTENTS

Changing Communities 4
Growing Up on the South Side 6
Making Mixtapes 8
Coloring Book 10
Becoming a Big Star 12
A Brighter Future 14
Chance the Activist 16
Starting SocialWorks 18
Spreading Joy and Raising Awareness 20
Glossary 22
For More Information 23
Index 24

CHANGING COMMUNITIES

Making a difference in the world often starts by making a difference in your community. Chance the Rapper knows this and is setting a good example for others to follow. He's one of the brightest stars in hip-hop music. He's made a big difference in that community as an independent artist—making his own music on his terms.

In addition, Chance is making a difference in the community he grew up in—the city of Chicago, Illinois. His music and his work in Chicago have lifted people up and **inspired** people to dream big. He has a powerful voice, and he's using to it help others.

In His Words

"There's a lot that just comes with betting on yourself."

— Interview with *Teen Vogue* magazine from May 2017

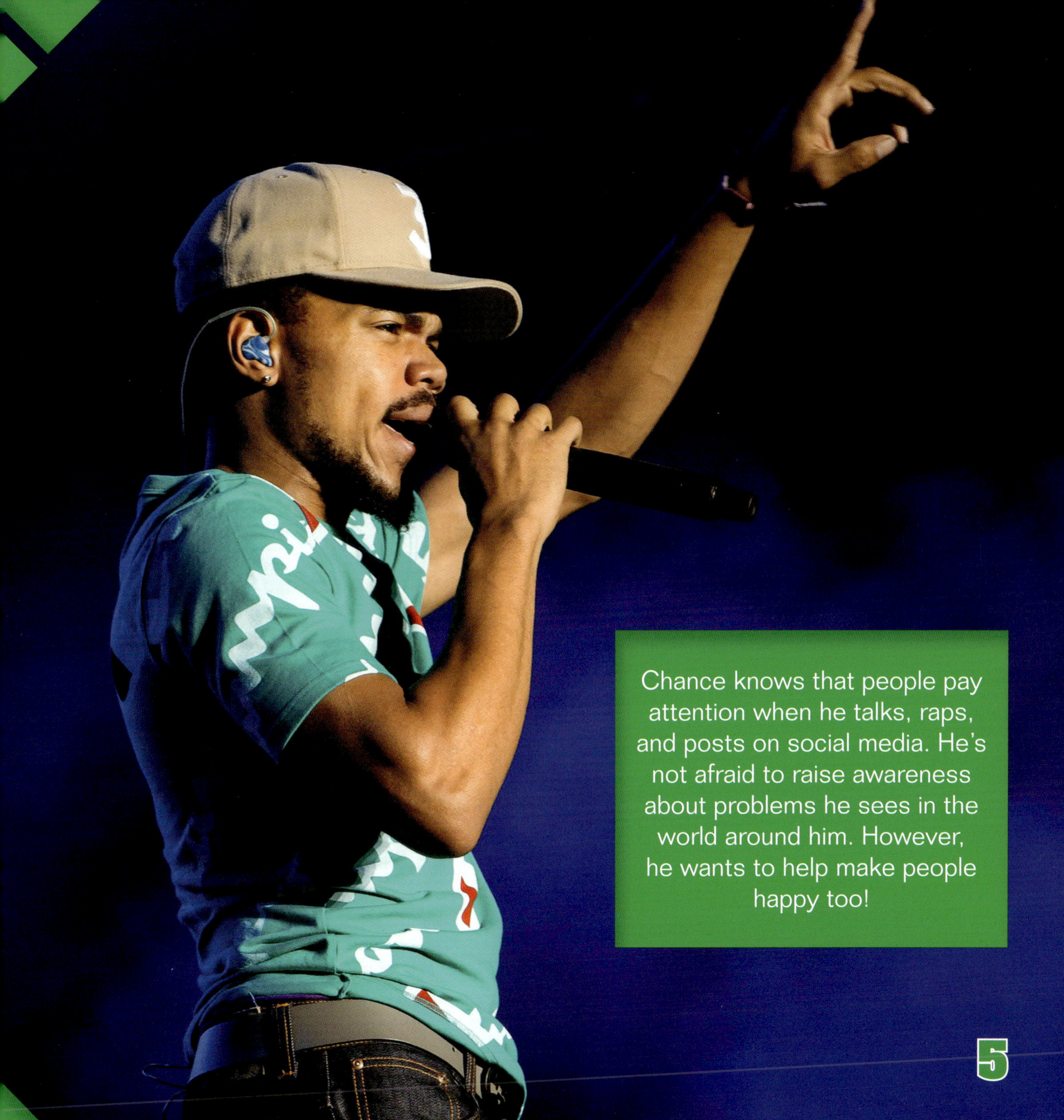

Chance knows that people pay attention when he talks, raps, and posts on social media. He's not afraid to raise awareness about problems he sees in the world around him. However, he wants to help make people happy too!

GROWING UP ON THE SOUTH SIDE

Chance the Rapper has always been a Chicago kid at heart. He was born on April 16, 1993, with the full name Chancelor Jonathan Bennett. Chance grew up on the South Side of Chicago, which is home to many Black families.

Chance grew up in a loving family, and his dad has always been an important part of his life. Chance's dad worked with Harold Washington, who was Chicago's first Black **mayor**. He also worked with Barack Obama when the president was a senator, or lawmaker, in Illinois. Chance's dad helped his son learn about politics, or ideas and plans for the government, at a young age.

In His Words

"I get my **personality** and my character and my understanding of … how I work with people and how I present my opinions—I get that from my dad."

— Interview with *GQ* magazine from February 2017

Chance has known Barack and Michelle Obama since he was a little kid! They've worked together over the years, and Barack has called Chance one of his favorite rappers.

MAKING MIXTAPES

Chance grew up listening to hip-hop. By the time he was in high school, he was making his own music. In 2012, he made a mixtape, or collection of music, called *10 Day*. He put it out on the music **streaming** service SoundCloud so people could listen to it for free.

The next year, Chance put out another mixtape on SoundCloud. *Acid Rap* became a huge hit, and the word quickly spread about this new voice in hip-hop. Chance worked with some big names on that mixtape, including Childish Gambino—the name the actor Donald Glover uses when he's making music.

In His Words

"It's not about the music being free ... It was always about the artist-to-fan relationship."

— Interview with *Billboard* magazine from 2016 about his mixtapes

Chance's mixtapes made him famous, but they didn't make him rich. Mixtapes often aren't sold the way regular albums are. Instead, they're a way for rappers to gain fans, who then spend money to see them on tour.

COLORING BOOK

Chance loved making music with other artists. In 2015, he was part of a group of artists called Donnie Trumpet and the Social Experiment that came out with a mixtape called *Surf*. The following year, Chance put out his next mixtape, called *Coloring Book*.

Coloring Book changed Chance's life. People loved that Chance didn't just rap about hard times; he **celebrated** life too. Chance won three Grammy Awards—the highest honor in music—after *Coloring Book* came out. He was the first artist to win a Grammy Award after only putting his music on streaming services.

In His Words

"You got to learn something new. You can't come in there and try and be the best. You got to come in there and become better."

— Interview with *The New Yorker* magazine from July 2020

Chance is an independent artist. He isn't signed to a **record label**, and he makes his music the way he wants to. He's inspired other independent artists to believe they can find success too.

BECOMING A BIG STAR

After years of making mixtapes, Chance released, or put out, his first album for people to buy in 2019. *The Big Day* was a big success, and it had a special story behind it. Chance said it was about the "big day" when he married his wife, Kirsten, earlier that year.

Chance had become a big star by 2019. He was in commercials for chips, candy, and many other things. He also hosted the popular late-night TV show *Saturday Night Live* in October 2019. In addition, he was the voice of a character called Bush Baby in the 2019 movie *The Lion King*.

In His Words

"I always wanted to be more of a person that people enjoy. Somebody that will make you laugh."

— Interview with *GQ* magazine from February 2017

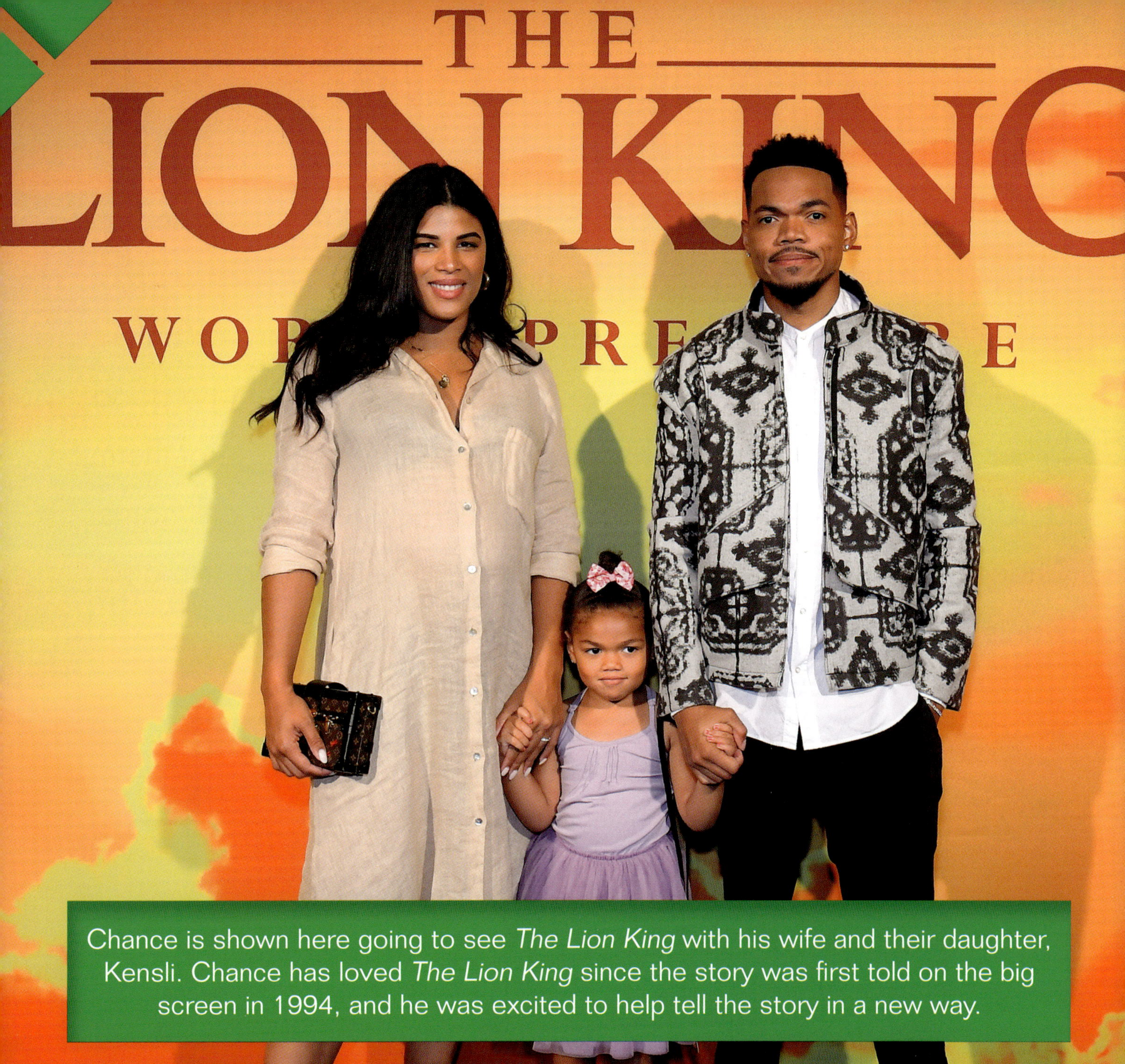

Chance is shown here going to see *The Lion King* with his wife and their daughter, Kensli. Chance has loved *The Lion King* since the story was first told on the big screen in 1994, and he was excited to help tell the story in a new way.

A BRIGHTER FUTURE

Chance was happy to be a part of *The Lion King* because he can share it with his kids. In 2015, his daughter Kensli was born, and in 2019, he and Kirsten welcomed another little girl—Marli.

Chance has talked openly about how important being a good father is to him. He loves his family and wants to take care of them. This includes taking care of the Chicago community they call home. Chance wants his kids to grow up in a safer, better world. He also wants this for all kids, especially all kids growing up in Chicago.

In His Words

"I've come to understand that art is awesome and beautiful because it's a **reflection** of life—but it's just a reflection, and the real thing is my daughter."

— Interview with National Public Radio (NPR) from August 2017

Chance is a strong voice in the fight to stop gun **violence** across the United States and especially in Chicago. He's shown here speaking out against gun violence in his hometown.

CHANCE THE ACTIVIST

One of the ways Chance is working to make a difference is by sharing his thoughts on politics. He believes in being educated about issues in his community and in the United States as a whole. He also believes in talking openly about those issues, especially with government leaders.

Chance's history with the Obama family has led him to help Barack Obama with different **programs**. For example, Chance has supported Barack's My Brother's Keeper Alliance. This is an effort to help young men of color succeed through methods such as matching them with mentors, or people they can look up to.

In His Words

"I think I am an activist at this point. I think that we should all be activists."

— Interview with *The New Yorker* magazine from July 2020

Chance is becoming known as an activist, or a person who fights for social and political change. He has strong opinions about politics, but he's also willing to learn more about opinions that are different from his own.

STARTING SOCIALWORKS

Chance has taken an even more hands-on approach to making a difference in Chicago. In 2016, he helped start SocialWorks. This is an **organization** that's working to help and inspire young people. Through this organization, he's raised millions of dollars for Chicago public schools.

SocialWorks has started programs to help in many areas of kids' lives, including education and **mental** health. It's also working to help with the problem of homelessness in Chicago. In addition, Chance knows how much the arts, such as music, helped him. That's why SocialWorks also has programs that show kids the power of writing and music.

In His Words

"Quality [good] education for public schools is the most important **investment** a community can make."

— Speech given in September 2017

The Life of Chance the Rapper

1993
Chancelor Jonathan Bennett is born on April 16 in Chicago.

2012
Chance puts out his first mixtape, *10 Day*.

2013
Chance puts out his second mixtape, *Acid Rap*.

2015
Chance works with Donnie Trumpet and the Social Experiment on the mixtape *Surf*, and his daughter Kensli is born.

2016
Chance puts out the mixtape *Coloring Book* and helps start SocialWorks.

2017
Chance wins three Grammy Awards.

2019
Chance's album *The Big Day* comes out, he gets married, his voice is in *The Lion King*, and his daughter Marli is born.

In less than 10 years, Chance went from being an unknown rapper to being one of the biggest stars in hip-hop!

SPREADING JOY AND RAISING AWARENESS

Chance has also become active in other causes that are close to his heart. He's spoken about the importance of the Black Lives Matter movement, which is working to call attention to the continuing problems of racism and police violence against Black Americans. He's also been a part of the #BlackBoyJoy movement on social media, which celebrates happiness shown by Black men.

Chance the Rapper believes in spreading joy, but that doesn't mean he **ignores** the problems around him. Instead, he's doing his part to fix those problems. He's making a difference through art and activism, and he's inspiring a lot of people along the way.

In His Words

"I'd be cool with people remembering me as a good, boring dude. As long as people say *good*."

— Interview with *GQ* magazine from February 2017

Be Like Chance the Rapper!

Learn about politics, and help the older people around you to learn more about the people and issues they're voting for.

Talk to your friends and family members about causes you care about.

Be proud of who you are and where you come from.

Raise money for your school or another cause you care about.

Find fun ways to help your community, such as cleaning up a park.

Write to government leaders about issues in your community.

Find a healthy way to express your thoughts and feelings. This can be through writing, music, drawing, or many other activities.

Chance the Rapper has done many things to make a difference in his community. These are some ways you can follow his example!

GLOSSARY

celebrate: To say that something is great or important.

ignore: To refuse to take notice of something.

inspire: To move someone to do something great.

investment: The act of putting something, such as time or money, into an effort in the hopes of getting something good back.

mayor: An official who is elected to be the head of the government of a city or town.

mental: Relating to the mind.

organization: A group formed for a specific purpose.

personality: The set of qualities and ways of behaving that make a person different from other people.

program: A plan under which action may be taken toward a goal. Also, a set of classes or events related to a certain subject.

record label: A company that signs artists to make music for them.

reflection: Something that shows the character of something else like an image in a mirror.

stream: To send music through the internet so a person can play it right away.

violence: The use of force to harm someone.

FOR MORE INFORMATION

WEBSITES

Chancelor Bennett: Grammy Awards

www.grammy.com/grammys/artists/chancelor-bennett

Chance the Rapper's page on the Grammy Awards website lists the Grammys he's won and fun facts about his life and music.

SocialWorks

www.socialworkschi.org/

The official SocialWorks website has facts about the different programs and events connected to this organization.

BOOKS

Cooke, Tim. *Barack Obama*. New York, NY: Gareth Stevens Publishing, 2019.

Hudalla, Jamie. *Chance the Rapper: Independent Master of Hip-Hop Flow.* North Mankato, MN: Capstone Press, 2020.

Niver, Heather Moore. *Chance the Rapper: Hip-Hop Artist.* New York, NY: Enslow Publishing, 2019.

INDEX

A

Acid Rap, 8, 19
activism, 16, 17, 20

B

Big Day, 12, 19
#BlackBoyJoy, 20
Black Lives Matter, 20

C

Chicago, Illinois, 4, 6, 14, 15, 18, 19
Coloring Book, 10, 19
commercials, 12

G

Glover, Donald, 8
Grammy Awards, 10, 19

I

independent artist, 4, 11

L

Lion King, The, 12, 13, 14, 19

M

mixtapes, 8, 9, 10, 12, 19
My Brother's Keeper Alliance, 16

O

Obama, Barack, 6, 7, 16

S

Saturday Night Live, 12
SocialWorks, 18, 19
SoundCloud, 8
Surf, 10, 19

T

10 Day, 8, 19